THE
ANALOGY
Of
SALES

THE ANALOGY Of SALES

Steven A Emerson

iUniverse, Inc.
New York Lincoln Shanghai

THE ANALOGY Of SALES

iUniverse books may be ordered through booksellers or by contacting:

iUniverse
2021 Pine Lake Road, Suite 100
Lincoln, NE 68512
www.iuniverse.com
1-800-Authors (1-800-288-4677)

ISBN-13: 978-0-595-34942-5 (pbk)
ISBN-13: 978-0-595-79655-7 (ebk)
ISBN-10: 0-595-34942-0 (pbk)
ISBN-10: 0-595-79655-9 (ebk)

Printed in the United States of America

Contents

FIELD GOAL KICKER

Kicking a football through the uprights of a field goal post looks pretty easy. I have watched hundreds of high school, college, and professional football games where field goal kickers run out onto the field and kick it. I actually went to a Thursday night middle school football game and saw a seventh grader kick a 35 yard field goal. As I was watching the game, my cell phone rang and it was a customer complaining about the pricing of his quote. After finishing the call with the customer, the kicker's father looked over and asked if I was in sales? I nodded and he proceeded to tell me how his brother is a salesman and it looked like an easy job to have. Of course he was never in sales, but as he said "What's so hard about getting in front of a customer and getting them to buy something he knows he needs?" I would think the same thing if I didn't do it for a living but I said "I guess you could say the same thing about a field goal kicker." "Your son just stands there, waits for the ball to be snapped, the holder puts the ball down, he takes two or three steps, and he kicks it." "Kicking a football looks pretty easy from where I am sitting". He looked puzzled with my comments and I didn't think explaining the similarities were going to do either of us any good. It was halftime and I got up to visit the concession stand.

But I will explain it to you.

It is 4th down with only three seconds to go in the game. His team is down by 2 points. It's a 35 yard field goal. The same distance the middle school kicker made. If he makes it, the team wins.

This should be an easy kick. The kicker wouldn't have gotten the job if he wasn't able to demonstrate to his coach, during try outs, that he could make it. The coach wouldn't put him out there if it was out of his range. It's only a 35 yard field goal. The goal post has the exact dimensions as the one on the practice field and 35 yards is the same distance on any football field.

You could come up with a hundred excuses why this kicker could have missed a 55 or 60 yard kick. Do you think there are as many excuses since it's just 35 yards? Unless the kicked was blocked, the only reason why a field goal kicker would miss a 35 yard field goal is if he choked. The pressure got to him and he missed it. Sure you could use the wind or field condition as an excuse, but its part of his job to consider those "intangibles" and adjust his kick accordingly. Another intangible could be a stadium full of people yelling and screaming. The possibility of winning the game and being the hero had to be on his mind as he stepped out on the field. The possibility of missing it and losing the game was on his mind too.

This is exactly what faces the sales person everyday. Our success and how we support our family and ourselves is by "kicking" everyday in the field. Take a minute and think of some of our "intangibles". We have customers who lose their budget, get fired, or start dating your competitor. We have service issues with our product and issues with our marketing department who are not able to get our product information out on time. We have engineering that can not get the proper software release out until the next quarter when we know the customer needs it today. Try using those "intangibles" as excuses on why you missed your quota more than once or twice. You get the same result as the kicker explaining his intangibles to his coach; a trip to the unemployment line.

I think our job is even more difficult than the field goal kicker because we have the last second field goal staring at us with every customer we face. In the course of a kicker's career, he may have 10 or 20 game winning kicks. In sales, every customer we face is a "sales winning kick". Finally, we have only one chance to win the deal. There are other game situations where a field goal kicker can miss it and have time to try again if his team can get the ball back. In sales, there is no second chance and every kick is our last with each customer. Here is another thing to think about as you realize how demanding your job is compared to a kicker.

Does the announcer mention the name of any of the other ten offensive players who are responsible for preventing the defense from blocking the kick? Does anyone even notice any of the offensive line? If the kicker misses it, the crowd and announcers know that it was only the kicker's fault. Everyone else did their job, but the kicker, whose only job was to kick that ball through the goal post, failed.

Your manager is not calling Joe in manufacturing to make sure that your product is built the way that your customer wants it. Mary in procurement has never been on a forecast call and asked about the shipment of raw materials. When it comes to your job as a salesperson, your manager and the rest of the team is just looking at you.

Mary and Joe will get their paycheck once a week for working 40 hours whether you sell something or not for now. But if you don't kick it through the uprights enough time, Mary and Joe could lose their job. They probably don't want to admit it, but their fate and livelihood is also based on you selling everyday. You have an incredible responsibility to yourself and your company to put it through the uprights. Never underestimate your value to your team and your responsibility.

VIVA LAS VEGAS

Las Vegas is excitement! Every temptation on this planet is within a 10 miles radius and with all its lights and beauty, it is asking you to forget your discipline, your common sense and just have fun. What Las Vegas can't help you with and takes no responsibility for is the consequences of just "having fun". This is especially true when it comes to my own greatest temptation: gambling. They entice us all with the big pay offs, a few "comps", and the idea that anyone can win. If you don't know this, let me be the first to tell you that Las Vegas expects you and 99% of everyone walking into the casino to lose. Las Vegas is a business and it wouldn't still be in business if there were more winners than losers. Your customer, just like Las Vegas, wants you to think that you have a chance of winning and your customer will entice you with ideas of the big sale and his future business. These ideas of the big commission check and the recognition of winning the big deal can sometimes take over common sense and good judgment. Your customer and Las Vegas expects to win every time and you have to accept that before you even walk in the casino or his office. The key to your success in both places is to control what you can afford to lose and establish your limits.

In an effort to ensure that I don't get caught up in a moment of "having fun" and put my daughter's college fund on number 21 on the roulette wheel, I establish a fixed dollar amount before I even get off the plane. I have a limit that I am prepared to gamble during my time in the casinos. I can play any game I want and at any limit. I have been to Las Vegas where I went right to the roulette wheel and put all my 200 dollars on red with the complete understanding that if I lost; I was going to bed early. If I wanted to spend more time down at the casino, I usually started at the $10.00 black jack table.

When you walk in a customer's office for the very first meeting, you should already be thinking what product you plan to sell him and the price. Maintaining limits at the very beginning will prevent you from doing things more reactively than rationally during the sales cycle. The idea that you "got a feeling" or feel "Lady Luck" is on your side has put more people in the poor house than the penthouse.

Your limits should also include the resources you have at headquarters to support your deal. This group usually includes your demo team, marketing, technical, and upper management. You need to dictate when you want to use these resources and respect them throughout the sales cycle. Just like in Las Vegas, there are several ways to gamble your money and just as many ways to divide your limit throughout the night. Don't get caught up or overreact to a customer who may make a general statement about having or needing something that may not be the right time in your opinion. Take a minute to understand their needs, just like time to understand the game of chance before you put your resource on the table.

Vegas can tempt you with the lights and the idea that you can win just as your customer can. They both need to do this to get your money and the best deal. You get caught up in the moment in Las Vegas and two minutes later, you can find yourself down a few thousand dollars having to explain to your spouse why there is some money missing from your checking account and a $25.00 ATM charge. If you get caught up in the moment and over react to the many "spontaneous" customers' demands, you basically lose control of the deal and your credibility among your teammates who are now wondering if you know what you are doing.

Going into a deal without setting limits with pricing and resources is basically allowing the customer to set the limits. The customer probably has bigger limits than you have resources and that's a game you can't afford to play. Set your limits before you walk into the office and you will be able to enjoy your time and actually beat the odds.

THE MORTGAGE

My mother is very successful as a real estate agent. She would say that her success in selling was not from years of selling houses, but her years LIVING in houses. My father was in the military and we moved several times. My mom got into real estate because we needed the money and who better to sell homes than someone who had both bought and lived in a lot of them. Also as a mother, it was easy to talk to potential homebuyers with children about the school districts and other "kids" things in the area. She knew the best grocery stores, the place to buy the kids shoes, and the closest dry cleaners. She knew a house's average electrical bill, the importance of showing where the cable connections were in the room, and she never left a bathroom without running the water and flushing the toilet.

She knew what customers should and would be looking for in a house. Her experience in selling homes made her understand that the house wasn't the only thing that needed to be sold. It was just as important to discuss the neighborhood, the schools, and the community where they would be spending just as much time living in.

If you were 19 years old, single, and living in an apartment, it would be hard to convince a home buyer with kids that you knew about the school district as a parent. You could go on the internet and pull the information from the website, but it would be difficult to tell the homebuyer about the PTA organization and that Ms. Gibbons would be a better 1st grade teacher for their son. Sure you can show them you passed the real estate test and have a certificate suitable for framing, but could you tell them what is the average water and electric bill for a

3,000 sq. ft. home? Best place to buy clothes for the children? Know a real good pediatrician?

So what can you do to overcome this and establish some credibility with your customer?

Anyone can learn about your product from the sales manual, but you also need to know how it will be used everyday. You need to look outside of the "brochure" and spend some time with actual customers. Find the time to see what it is like to use your product. There are some products that you will sell that will be difficult or impossible to demonstrate or use. This is where talking to your install base or customer with your product is essential. Find the time to talk to users and get their perspective. If you sell a product that you can self demo or try out yourself, make it a point to "try it out" in order to see it the same way as a customer who uses it everyday.

This could be the customer's first time buying a large ticket item. Certain deals can be worth hundreds of thousands of dollars. The software on these systems alone cost more than what it would cost to send his kid to college for 4 years. The more you understand what they are going through and their needs beyond the equipment that they are buying, the better you will be able to help them through the "sticker" shock.

During the sales cycle, you may have the opportunity to take customers to visit a site that has your product. This will allow them to get a chance to talk to actual users and see your product performing live. Begin to establish a relationship with these sites before taking customers to visit. Spend time with them and feel comfortable in their surroundings. Understand how they are using the product and how it could be better. I always made it a point to stop by my install base once a month to spend some time to learn more about my product. I also made it a point when I came to bring lunch to the staff. By establishing a strong relationship with your install base and feeling comfortable at the site, your confidence in the product and the ability to understand your future customer's questions from their perspective will increase. This will allow you to have a better appreciation for the value of your product and what the customer needs to see during the visit.

You don't have to be a home owner to sell a house, but knowing "why" some one wants a house and their needs beyond the four walls and two door garage can help you sell more, establish credibility and keep you out of the poor house.

LAWYER

I once heard a lawyer say that you should always know the answer to any question you ask a witness. I think I can understand that for a couple of reasons. The first is the jury knows what side the lawyer is on, but the lawyer needs to make sure his witnesses can come in and support his case. This allows the lawyer to get his point across to the jury and makes his case more credible. The second reason is a lawyer would never ask a question to his witness without telling them before they got on the stand what he was going to ask. Lawyers always meet with their witnesses to review their testimony prior to them taking the witness stand. Could you imagine what would happen to the credibility of a lawyer and his case if he asked a question to a witness who didn't know the answer or didn't expect the question? It would certainly cause some hesitation by the jury to believe either the lawyer or the witness.

The jury is the only group that is going to decide the verdict. More times than not, a verdict by a jury is based more on testimony from a witness than the opening or closing remarks of a lawyer. The key to being a successful lawyer is to know when to ask those questions and when to pick the right witness to take the stand. The key to being a successful salesperson is to know when to ask the right questions with the right people available to answer them.

When you are selling to a group of people, you are just like a lawyer. Each person who is part of the decision making process is a jurist. They know what side you are on. They have heard you in presentation after presentation discussing why your product is the best, but just like the jury in a trial, your customers want it reinforced with your witnesses.

The "witnesses" in your sales cycle can come from a variety of sources. They can be existing customers that may have agreed to take customer calls to provide some insight to your product. You may have your marketing manager or a product engineer present a more formal presentation on the future product roadmap or discuss the more technical aspect of your product. You may also have a demo person come in to show the product to the group giving the customer more opportunities to see the product in action.

These are your "witnesses" and your responsibility. Just like a witness going on to the stand, they have to be fully prepared to discuss and answer questions you have provided them. Additionally, they need to know what the competing lawyer is saying to better prepare their "testimony". You should not let them get on the witness stand or in front of your customer without making sure you know exactly what they are going to say and how they are going to say it. You are setting them up for failure and you as well, if you do not take the time to review with them your strategy and objectives of your meeting.

Your manager and others may think that they know it all and do not need to be bothered with an explanation on how to handle the customer. You should make every effort to "prep" them before they meet your customer. Be professional and respectful of their position in the company and their time to help you, but make absolutely sure they have talked to you and you have informed them with exactly what you want to accomplish. A simple e mail, a short conversation as you are going over to see the customer or a phone call to explain the situation will put you in a better position and cover yourself if something doesn't go as planned.

On certain occasions you may not need your manager coming to the meeting. Just like a lawyer in a trial, you want to make sure you use the right witness at the right time. Stay objective with your manager and ensure him if he is needed, you will give him a call.

Take the time to prep your witnesses to be their best in front of the jury. This is your case and though the witness may have some interest in how the verdict comes out, you are ultimately responsible. I can guarantee you that after explaining to your boss why your witnesses were not prepared to testify and you lose the deal, you will be the only one found guilty and spending time in solitary confinement at the jailhouse with no chance of parole.

MODEL GLUE

When I was a kid, I use to build model planes. You could buy the plane unassembled with some glue and paint at any general store. Once I got home, I would race to my room and clear off my dresser to begin the building of the greatest plane on the block. Ignoring the directions, I began gluing every piece of my model plane together. Having spent only 15 minutes working on it (the maximum amount of time I would spend on any project that didn't have a joy stick), my final result was a plane that only loosely resembled the plane on the box, but one I was convinced was ready to fly. Had I read the directions, I would have realized that the plane needed to sit for a few hours to allow the glue to bind to all the pieces. I assumed that if I used more glue, it would hold longer and quicker. By the time I was done, I had used the entire tube of glue. The glue was not only layered on the plane, but on my hands, my clothes, the four clean socks I got from the dresser to clean the glue off the dresser, and on anything 10 feet inside the "building" zone.

With my "modified" rendition of a fighter plane, I raced to my friend's house to play. Less than 30 feet from my house, the plane's tail had fallen off (lost in the grass to be eaten by my dog). After a few steps more, I noticed the wings hanging on only by the "spider web" of glue stretching to maintain a connection to the plane's base. The plastic pilot inside, had he been alive, would have died of glue fumes by now while frantically making an effort to eject (impossible of course because of the amount of glue used to hold him in).

When I finally got to my friend's house, he was playing basketball while waiting for the glue on his plane to dry. I dropped my plane and began to play basketball with him. A few hours later, he was playing with a plane fully intact. I was resolved to using what was left of my plane...Imagination is great.

The point is that my friend followed the directions and waited for the glue to dry. He recognized that he had to give the glue time to stick to the pieces. He also used the right amount of glue. The amount I used was enough to glue an actual 747. By using the right amount, on the right places, the glue was able to bound and "stick" to the plane.

Your product information is the model glue. Your customer will provide you the directions they need to build their plane. They will "direct" you with the information that they need to make the decision. Your job is to make sure you provide the right amount of information to the right places. Too much in the wrong place will only make it sticky and difficult to use.

Your customer can only take so much information and just like the plane, it only needs a certain amount of glue. Make it a point to offer your information "proportionally" to both their ability to comprehend and retain it. Too much information at the wrong time can be disastrous. You can confuse the customer and this confusion can lead to more questions that could potentially jeopardize your credibility. Your customer is smarter than you and if you don't believe it, just ask them. It's your fault, in their mind, if the information you provided is either too much or can't be understood. A simple test I use is the "five hour" test. Take any information you created to send to a customer and put it in your office drawer for five hours. After five hours, pull it out and have a friend read it. If your "home office" is close to one of your kid's rooms, ask them to read it. If it makes sense to your friend or kids, then you can send it to your customer. If not, you probably need to work on it. In most cases, your customer will take at least a day or two to find the time to review your information. Your customer will also need time to gather information from your competition and may "put" your information away or just toss it on his "to do" pile. If you provide your information in a clear and concise manner, he should be able to understand it whenever he can get to it.

Make every attempt to present your information in person. Faxes, e-mails, or traditional mail are great methods in getting information from one place to another, but it limits your ability to ensure they have it and more importantly understand it. It also gives you an excuse to stop by and get an opportunity to meet the other people who are part of the decision making process.

Providing the right information at the right time with the intent of supporting your customer's request will allow your sales to fly above the clouds.

FIREMAN

Sometimes the hardest thing to do as a salesperson is to ask for the business. You have spent months with this customer and have developed a great business relationship. However there are some occasions where you have also developed a personal relationship as well. There is no question that this friendship can provide some advantages in working with the customer, but it also has the potential to cause problems if given priority over the business relationship. The time put into your deal and consequences of losing it can make anyone a little hesitant and anxious to ask for the business because you don't want to hear you lost the deal. Rejection is something we all want to avoid with both our friends and customers. However sales rejection is something you need to accept and embrace as part of your job. Don't take it personally because the customer's business needs should always have priority over his need in keeping you as a new best friend. His only responsibility, in regards to your relationship, is to buy the right product and you always need to remind yourself that his job depends on it. Your responsibility is to establish a relationship of trust and respect in order to sell your product. If you allow or promote a friendship with the customer that goes beyond a professional one, it is your responsibility to ensure the customer always knows you are there as a salesperson first and not someone who needs another friend to add to the Christmas card list. Make sure your customer expects you to work for his business and at the appropriate time, ask for his commitment that you are his vendor of choice. A good way to always keep this in mind is to think of a fireman.

You are in a hotel conference room having your quarterly business review meeting with your team. You are in a room with no windows and all you have been looking at for the last two hours is the same power point presentation created last quarter with just different numbers. The background isn't even different. This is the one that tells you that your business wants you to sell more of the same product to the same customers in the same territory for 20 percent more than you offered them last quarter.

As you are reaching for the candy on the table and wondering when or if the snacks are coming, your best friend comes into the room and says there is a fire. Everyone in the room looks at each other and their first question is "who is this guy?" You know who he is, but he doesn't work for the hotel and you are thinking to yourself why he is here. You explain to everyone that even though he is not a fireman, he is your friend and the group should leave. No one expects your friend to help put out the fire or save them. Most would think it was nice of him to stop and warn the group of the fire. So everyone gets up and walks out leaving the power point presentation to be burned to the ground.

What if you were in the same situation but instead of your friend, the person was a fireman. He is wearing a fire jacket, has on a fire helmet and is carrying an axe. With a fireman telling you there was a fire, you would not think twice about getting up. This person is dressed as a fireman, he has the equipment of a fireman, and wouldn't be asking you to get out if there wasn't a fire. As opposed to your friend, it is the fireman's responsibilities to make sure you are safe and that the fire is put out. The fireman would only be there if there was a fire and he is trained to put out fires and save lives…and in this case…yours. Finally, your expectations are higher and more specific for the fireman than your friend. Your friend just happened to be there to help and stopped by to just "warn you", while the fireman came with a specific purpose to save lives and put out fires. You never doubted the reason the fireman was there, did you? When the "smoke" clears, you may go over and thank the fireman for the effort and saving your life. You may even strike up a conversation and find things you have in common. But whatever comes from your "after the fire" conversation, neither of you would doubt that the reason why you met in the first place was because he was doing his job first.

When you walk into the customer's office, does he think for a minute you are there to be his best friend? Do you really think that he is sitting around waiting for you to come to his office and talk about your summer vacation? Do you think he set up an appointment with you to talk about the new dog or your kid's teachers? In the years of selling, have you ever received a "personalized" letter from any of your customers unless he was asking for donations to support the new wing of the hospital or their kid's soccer fundraiser campaign? Just like the fireman walking into your meeting, you are dressed like a salesman, carrying your "equipment" for your presentation like a salesman, and giving him your business card that reads "salesman" not "best friend" on it. Your customer doesn't doubt that you are a salesman, so why should you? You met the fireman because he was there to save your life. You met your customer because you have a product you want him to buy.

Making "small talk" is natural and should be expected, but keep it very general in order to easily transition into the real reason why you are in his office. Don't try and hide behind a friendship and use that as a way to get the customer to buy your product. It shows lack of respect to the customer's primary responsibility and demonstrates your inability to perform your job as it is intended. Make a point to respect his role and expect the same from your customer. Just like the fireman, you have a job to do and you wouldn't be there if you couldn't get it done. If your keep this in mind, no one will get burned.

THE SIXTY FOUR THOUSAND DOLLAR QUESTION

I saw this guy at a convention who claimed he could take any book and tell you what a word was on any page. He asked for a volunteer in the crowd to pick a page from their book, then find a word, show it to the audience (but not him), and close the book. We all waited. He told us he would ask a series of questions to the volunteer to determine the word. At question 25, I got bored and left. At that point, I didn't care. I just lost interest and felt that I wasted a half hour of my life.

People don't want to be asked a lot of questions and certainly don't want to answer questions that serve no purpose to their needs. Remember there is a difference between a conversation and an interrogation. I always hated coming home after a date because my mom would be waiting up for me. The "interrogation" started before I shut the door. Some of the standard opening questions were, but not limited to: "Where did you go?", "Who were you with?", and "Why didn't you call so I could tell you we needed milk?". All I got in answering her first question was three more and not once did she ask if I had a good time. Just like the guy at the convention, my answers only brought more questions that eventually bored me and even made me angry.

There are some training classes that tell you to ask questions to get the customer to talk. The problem is that if you don't ask the right questions, you will have them talking about things that you don't need to know. Make sure your questions have something to do with getting him to select your product or understanding the sale cycle. I have been in situations where I was not prepared and after I introduced myself, asked a question just to break the roaring silence. I asked the most volatile question of them all; the "How was your weekend" question. After an hour of hearing about the camping trip, the customer was both out of time to tell me more about his weekend and time to talk about my product (which was the only reason I should have been there). I learned a lot about camping and he learned nothing about my product. Never ask a question that you are not prepared to listen to the complete answer and never assume your simple questions will lead to a simple and short answer from your customer.

Customers know what they want to tell you, but they don't want to be interrogated. They probably have been waiting for this meeting to review their needs before you even walked in. Don't mix this time up or confuse the customer by asking questions that steer away from the customer's objective. Customers want you to be interested in their business needs and want to take time to explain them. If you need to ask a question, it should allow the customer the opportunity to focus on how excited they are in getting a new product and the way it will make them more successful. Your responsibility is to make sure they are talking about what you want and need to hear in order to win the deal. Buying your product to make them successful is a topic that the customer should want to discuss and one in which you need to listen. There can be another time to hear about the camping trip after celebrating the customer's commitment to buy your product.

Before I go into the customer's office for the first time, I have four questions to ask the customer. Sometimes the meeting last two hours and sometimes it last only 30 minutes. Remember it is not how long you were there but what was said to help you win the deal. Keep in mind that most sales cycles last months and you will be meeting with the customer many times to discuss the deal. Make it a point to spend the appropriate time to gather your information and then leave. In most cases, these questions have ensured that I provided the customer the ability to talk about what I needed to hear and what he wanted to say: Every sales person should have a set of standard questions to ask. Going in without a set of questions and objectives is like going on a trip without a map. These questions provide the customer the ability to talk about the two most important topics: Your product and his needs. Nothing else matters in this setting.

1.   How will my product help this customer meet their objectives?

2.   Who does this customer report to and what are their expectations of this product?

3.   How is my company seen in the customer's mind (Remember the customer needs to trust you and the company. You need to reinforce your company's commitment to the product)?

4.   What is their time frame regarding the sales cycle and what are their expectations of our working relationship?

These are some of the questions that I usually use, but the objective is to ask questions that allow the customer to talk and provide you the information you need regarding this deal. Anyone can get the right answer if they can ask enough questions, but if you ask the right questions first, you won't have to guess the "right word" from your customer's book. He will tell you......but you have to just ask him the right way.

25 FLAVORS

A new ice cream store opened up in our neighborhood when I was 12 years old. One night after dinner, the family jumped into the Grand Safari station wagon with the wood panels to get some ice cream.

This was the first ice cream store I went into that had more than five flavors. The counter was wall to wall refrigerators. There were 25 flavors in all. Some were the basic flavors that you would see at the grocery store. Then there were the "unusual" flavors like grape and bubble gum. It was hard to keep up with all the choices, but we were next in line and it was time to order.

My youngest brother Jeffrey decided to go with the grape ice cream. He based his choice on the fact that a few of his "cool" friends tried it and thought it was the best. Jeff wanted to be seen as one of the "cool" kids and thought by getting the same flavor as them, he would be able to fit in. My other brother Russell went with Bubble Gum ice cream. In his mind, it was a great combination of two things that he loved; ice cream and bubble gum. How could you go wrong with combining two great things that you can eat as once? Both decisions were quick, decisive, and without hesitation. It was my turn next and the kid working there asked what I wanted. I needed to make a choice and I needed to make it now.

But confused with all the choices, I was lost and had no idea what flavor to chose. The kid working there was getting frustrated and kept saying "Come on, pick one". I heard the crowd behind me telling me what to get and my father was losing his patience.

What if I didn't like it? I didn't want to waste my choice on something I didn't like. Why didn't I just get what my brothers got? They seemed to like their choice and I wanted something I would like too. I knew I had only one choice and I had to make it now. I finally made my choice....Vanilla ice cream in a waffle cone.

There were 24 other flavors and I picked vanilla. The kid working the counter almost leaped over the counter to hit me. My father asked if I was sure and my brothers just laughed.

When I got the ice cream, I went to my seat with the family. I still heard people who waited in line behind me talking about my choice. "Can you believe that kid ordering vanilla?"? "Why did he take so long to pick just vanilla?"? My family was enjoying their ice cream while I ate in silence still a little embarrassed about my choice. My mother asked how my ice cream was and I told her it was the best vanilla that I ever had. I offered her a bite.

Your customers will have several choices, but will only make one decision. This is a luxury that competition provides us. Though it is nice to have, competition can also make it more difficult for a customer to make a final choice and stick to it. It is not easy to make the "big decision" and we need to respect the responsibility the customer has in making it. If my brothers did not like their choice, they would ask my dad for another pick. My father would remind them that they had their one choice and now had to live with it. My brothers would get angry, throw it away, and make sure to never pick it again.

There is not a trash can big enough to throw away a big piece of equipment and your customer will never have enough money to buy another one to fix his "bad choice". We also need to understand that your customers are getting pressure from other people to make their decision.

Your customer may be pressured by some of the "cool" kids to purchase what they have. Peer pressure does not end in high school and no one wants to be seen by their peers as the guy who made the wrong decision. He may have one of your competitors, who sells a variety of different products that your customer is already using, telling him that you like my other products and there is no reason you won't like this one. The competitor making the "bubble gum flavor" point: How can you go wrong with purchasing this product when the other product you have of mine is doing great? He may have a boss who is telling him he has to make a decision soon because he is delaying other projects that coordinate with his decision.

Make your product "vanilla". Make it simple to understand and trust. Make your features and benefits meet the customer's needs. Develop a trust and build the customer's confidence that regardless of what every one else says, this is the best product you can buy. My mom took a bite of my vanilla ice cream and said it was the best she ever had. She recognized I was a little embarrassed about my pick and people were laughing at me. She made a point to let me know my pick was the best.

Be there to support your customer even after the sale. Go to his office and tell him you both appreciate his business and the trust he had in you. Make it a point to send a thank you letter or even have your boss give him a call. This customer picked you over all the other vendors out there.

You can never go wrong with vanilla no matter how many flavors there are out there just as you can never go wrong with good old fashion selling. A handshake, a commitment to your product, enthusiasm in presenting your product, and showing respect for the role and responsibility the customer has in making his choice is just as simple as vanilla ice cream. And it taste great!

GRAND MA

Why do customers complain to sales people? The obvious answer, for someone who has never sold before, is the sales person did something wrong. Yet in some cases, we get in situations where it may not be our fault but we are the first person the customer wants to reach out to complain. The question is how do we handle these customer's complaints without jeopardizing our credibility or mitigating the customer's problem.

My Grand Ma complains about everything. She complains about the weather and complains that her coffee is too cold. She complains that people drive too fast and that I drive too slow getting her to the mall. Once in the mall, she complains about how expensive everything is and then after walking around for an hour, wants to leave to go to the drug store where she has a coupon for shampoo. I try to avoid her whenever she comes to the house…My mother is not so lucky but has a way of dealing with her.

My mother tends to coddle her by agreeing with her while trying to fix all her complaints. This usually works for a little while, but you can't change the weather and you can never get the coffee "just right". You act like this with a customer and they will always ask for more. Why shouldn't they? If you keep on agreeing with them, they will keep on expecting you to agree with them especially later in the sales cycle when they say your price is too high. Every time you agree, you are giving them permission to go farther down their list of complaints and expecting to get what they want.

My grandfather, a true saint by anyone's account, just ignores her. He blocks her out either by leaving the room or using the remote control to raise the volume on the television. My grandfather is a plumber and probably would not be a good salesman. If you walk out on a customer, you are walking away from your livelihood. "Raising" the volume by tuning them out may make them forget their complaints for a while, but they will come back to haunt you later in the sales cycle when you may not have as much time to resolve them.

My wife is the best at this and I think it has to do with the fact that we still have small children. The complaining that my two year old does is no different than my Grand Ma...except for one thing...when my Grand Ma complains about the food, she tells us in words. When my two year old wants to complain about the food, he starts to cry. Whether it's crying or using words, both just want someone to hear them and take care of whatever problem they have. One cant use words so he cries, the other one is too old to cry, so she uses words. My wife's main objective is to take the time to understand what is exactly wrong and makes sure she can help.

Customers can be like my Grand Ma or my two year old. They want attention and you are the only person they can go to when anything, even remotely associated with your product, goes wrong. They may want to complain because they claim they did not get enough training for their group (even though you trained everyone when they first bought your product and now everyone that was originally trained on the product has quit). He is threatening you because of the lack of use of the product you sold him (It isn't your fault the factory that supported 10,000 jobs is closing down). He is calling his attorney because he heard from another customer that they received a better price (It's not your fault that the customer bought during a promotion). In all these situations, you are the focal point for these and all their complaints. Sometimes they will come out and tell you the problem just like my Grand Ma. They tell you exactly what is wrong regardless if you can fix it or not. Other times they can be like my two year old and just "cry" about your product with the hope you can figure it out and fix it. Make it clear that you are there to listen and help if possible. Establish your role and your intention to support your customer's needs. Be specific and upfront with the customer. "Tell me your problem with my product and service and let me understand completely what the problem is". Get them to stop "crying" and confusing their issues with other things that are outside your control.

Always stay professional and never subject yourself to topics that go outside your responsibility as a salesperson or make you feel uncomfortable. You are neither a target for your customer's abuse because he had a bad day and needs to just "vent" or a psychologist, political pundit, or priest. Your personal opinion on issues not relating to your business is something that should be kept out of any conversation with a customer.

Finally, your customers have another thing in common with all of us: they can have a bad day. Don't take it personally if the customer doesn't want to see you or isn't as "happy" as he usually is when you meet. He could have heard that his kid just wrecked his favorite car, his wife lost her credit card, his assistant just quit, or his Grand Ma is coming over for dinner. Make the right decision and when you think it is a bad time, ask to reschedule. You don't want to be remembered by your customer as the sales guy in the office when some "bad news" came his way.

PLAY-DOH

There are certain deals where more than one person is involved in the decision making process. They will tell you one person is the decision maker, but the other people in the group have a personal interest in this decision and wouldn't be there if they didn't care or have an opinion. More times than not, it's actually the other members of the group that will use the product that the decision maker selects and it is important that you keep these "users" engaged and excited about your product throughout the sales cycle.

The first time you usually meet the whole group is at the first sales presentation. When you are in that meeting, try to think of Play-Doh.

Is it possible to open the five canisters of Play-Doh and make the banana split you see on the box? Absolutely, but you only have one chance to build your banana split. Your one chance is based on the fact that once you start creating your masterpiece and putting together all those different colors together, it is impossible to break it up and put it all back into its original canisters when you are done. How in the world does anyone play with this stuff more than once before the five different colors all look like dark orange? Have you ever ended up with the same amount of Play-Doh that you started with when you first began to create your banana split?

In your first meeting you have the opportunity to introduce yourself to the group and learn what their role is both within the organization and the purchasing decision. Their real job, within the group or organization, is usually easy to figure out. Most employees wear name tags or at the very least will have business cards. However, their role in the decision making process is more difficult and you have to keep focused to find this out. Everyone is important. Each has a different color with a different purpose and objective. Also your banana split will need more white clay for the vanilla ice cream and less red clay for the cherries on top: different amounts, but each amount contributing to the perfect creation. The objective is to find out whom (what color) and how much time (how much Play-Doh) you have to spend with each person to win the deal. A good place to start is at the first meeting.

Take the time in the meeting to watch how the group talks and the questions they ask. Here are a few rules: (1) the more interested someone is, the most active he will be in the process. (2) the one that is standoffish is usually the one that wants more control, but recognizes that he will have to live with whatever is selected. (3) the negative one is usually the one that either has a relationship with your competition or just wants to be confrontational. Each customer is like a different color of Play-doh; each with their special place and amount to create your masterpiece.

In this meeting, they may want you to think that they all are the same, but they are as different as the colors of Play-doh. They want you to see dark orange because in that room, they want you to feel that when you are talking to one, you are talking to them all. No smart customer will ever debate or argue with a fellow group member in front of you. This is where you have to watch and make some judgment calls on where to begin after the meeting. The rule of thumb is to make your first call to the group leader. This is the best place to start and where you will end up at the end of the sales cycle discussing price.

You never have the same amount of Play-Doh after you create your masterpiece and begin putting it away. Each visit to the customer should allow you to "take away" something to use to win the deal.

During the course of your meetings, you will begin to gather information you need and where to go to get more. You want to avoid two things as you are building your creation. The first is spending too much time with the people who have given you all the support they can provide. Respect them and their opinion, but too much red and not enough white will not make the perfect banana split. Secondly, try and avoid jumping from one member to another everyday. It is both unprofessional and gives people a feeling that you don't know what you are doing. A better approach is to occasionally make "surprise" visits. This allows you a chance to catch the customer in a different setting and provides you a little more control.

The banana split is not complete without all the colors being the right proportion and in the right place. Make it a point to remember this and you will have a great masterpiece you can share with your boss.

THE SQUIRREL

I have a home office with a window where I can look out to see my backyard. I find myself watching the squirrels while I am on the phone listening to one of my reps explaining why he needs a lower price for a deal or a customer complaining about something. The other day I noticed a squirrel walking across the thinnest branch of a tree. I watched him reach the end of the branch and, without hesitation, he leaped over to the other tree. What was incredible was the squirrel didn't stop for a moment to think about the jump. Where did the squirrel get the confidence to "just" leap? I wonder if he ever thought about falling and if he did about his certain death. I bet I spent more time thinking about that squirrel falling then he did. I also know that the only thought that squirrel ever had was getting to the other branch because at the time, it was the only thing that mattered.

Television shows and books tell us all about people who overcame great adversities and "leaped". The one common denominator that all these people have, whether big or small, was the need to just leap to the other side. In some cases, the biggest problem they had with leaping to the other side was other people telling them that they couldn't do it. From the discovery of the speed of light to fighting for civil rights, great people have been faced with narrow minded people who created a world of thinking and perception that was based on nothing but what they thought was right. The leapers of the world were able to overcome these people because they focused on what they needed to get done and their only goal was to get to the other side.

Your body "leaps" to the other side everyday. Take for example your red blood cells. All they do is race through your body carrying oxygen. Your white blood cells are fighting bacteria and viruses even as you read this line. These parts of your body do their respected jobs every second of your life handling every adversity it faces with little regard for anything that cannot contribute to its function. White blood cells are not worrying about missing your quota. Red blood cells are not worrying whether your boss likes you. Why should you spend your time thinking or worry about things that can not make you successful? Try to hold your breath for 20 minutes. You can't because your body won't let you. As soon as you pass out, the brain will take over and get your lungs to start working. The brain knows what it has to do to jump start your body even if you try to stop it. What conscious thoughts are you thinking to stop you from being great? Are you thinking about getting to the other side or hoping that you don't fall?

The conscience mind that allows you to think the bad thoughts and worries that you create in your head really make life miserable for the remaining 99% of your body. It is like an extra 100 pound weight to have to carry on your back for your leap. It is not easy to avoid some people's "view" of the way they think you should be and what they think it takes to be great. Take a minute and watch TV. There are enough commercials telling us we are too fat, we don't have enough hair, or our kids hate us to make us question what we have ever done right. While standing in line at the grocery stores, take a look at the magazines at the check out stand. The magazines are lined with beautiful women and men with articles telling us we could look just like them. My favorite articles are about the movie stars who complain how hard parenting is when they only have three nannies, a cook, and a driver! My white blood cells could never handle the "bacteria and viruses" that my mind has to battle with everyday.

The squirrel and your entire body is not thinking about failing or being inadequate. The squirrel is not worrying about what other squirrels think about his hair, his figure, his kids, or his home. The squirrel is only thinking about eating and bringing food to his nest. This is his responsibility in order to survive and be successful. Those commercials and magazines with beautiful people on the covers are telling you the way they want you to be. These thoughts should never enter your head nor do they have anything to do with you surviving and being successful. Your body isn't thinking about the hair you lost, how much you weigh, or the color of your eyes.

Take a lesson from your body and the squirrel. Do your job and be proud of it. Focus on the successful, both through triumph and failure. Be glad you are in the game, with a chance to play and make a difference. Jump to the tree everyday and remember the only people telling you that you can't, are the ones that wish they had the courage to reach the other side.

SPY CAMERA

When I was a kid, I would get a dollar from my father for helping in the yard on Saturday mornings. I would ride my bike down to the convenience store and buy a candy bar, an orange soda, and a comic book. Every comic book I ever bought had advertisements for things like magic tricks and super balls that could bounce over a large building. These ads are similar to the ones we see in the magazines at the grocery store or bookstores. The "how to" ads to lose weight and make more money are designed with the same intention as the ads in my comic books 25 years ago; to sell their product by creating high expectations.

The spy camera in my comic book looked like a great investment. It was small and I could sneak it into school. The pictures on the ad were fantastic. The idea of being able to take pictures without anyone noticing gave me the thoughts of being a detective or spy. I imagined myself walking to school with my camera, coming across a robbery, taking a picture of a criminal, and becoming a hero.

A few weeks later I received the camera and after taking pictures of everything from the moon to my dog, I went to the grocery store to get them developed. When I got them back, they were all dark and out of focus. Why were my pictures not the same as the ones in the ad? I looked at the ad again and noticed the fine print. The fine print stated that a professional took the pictures and that results may vary. I created my own expectations of what the camera should do and overlooked the obvious fact that the camera can only be as good as the one taking the picture. It is also true that the professional photographer took more than one picture in order to find the perfect one for the ad.

Everyday of your customer's life he is bombarded with "spy camera" ads. If it is not on TV, it is on billboards. If it is not on the radio, it is on magazine covers in the grocery store. If its not his kid walking in with their comic book showing him the ad on the back cover, it is you going in there saying your product can do everything he wants.

These ads do not come with sales people to explain the product. The ads only have a few testimonials with the fine print "results may vary". These ads usually have a P.O box number and an 800 number that no one answers. They can afford these ads because if the customer is upset, it is almost impossible to reach them to get their money back. You don't have that opportunity to hide or avoid calling the customer back. In order to avoid those angry phone calls from customers who expected more from your product after they bought it, start working with your customer before they buy it to explain exactly what your product can do and the customer's responsibility to make it work.

Be clear when discussing and demonstrating the technical features of your product. Make it a point during a demonstration to show these features to your customer but remember your customers are not as experienced in using your product as you or your demo person. If you use demo people to come in to demonstrate your product they will have extensive training and experience with your product. As your demo person is making it look easy with a few simple "key strokes", remind your customer that proper and sufficient training is essential to use the product in the same manner. Avoid using the "it's very simple" or "anyone can learn it" comments as the demo person is reviewing the product's features. Be respectful towards the demo person regarding their knowledge of your product and remember if it was so easy, why did you have to bring the demo person in to help?

Don't make this conversation with the customer sound like a warning. Turn it into a selling point on your training and your commitment to support the customer in getting the most from your product. This will establish your credibility in the customer's mind and a gentle reminder in the future if he decides not to get the proper training.

The most expensive product your customer will ever buy is the one he can't use. Take the time to take the right picture of the customer's needs and in the right light. Make it a priority to spend time talking about the entire product and its features, even the more technical ones. Providing the right expectations to the customer, including all the features and benefits of your product will make a happy customer smile and say "cheese".

WILD BILL MARINE

I went to Officer Candidate School (OCS) to be an officer in the Marine Corps. One of the many things I had to do while I was there was to ensure that my equipment was clean at all times. Every Friday morning the platoon would have weekly inspection in order to ensure that we kept our equipment clean and functional. If you failed this inspection, you would be forced to stay on base and clean your equipment over the weekend. This would mean no weekend pass, no chance for any good food, and no chance of seeing your girlfriend or wife. I remember the very first inspection and how I told myself that I had to make sure I was prepared.

It was Thursday night before the first inspection, the rest of the platoon and I were up the entire night and into the early morning making sure our weapon and the rest of our equipment was clean. Everyone was working hard to get ready except for Wild Bill, who was in his rack (bed) by 10 PM. Most of the platoon looked at Wild Bill and noticed how quickly he was able to get his equipment ready. At this point, I didn't care about anyone but myself but didn't understand how Wild Bill could be prepared. I was cleaning my rifle making sure every part of it shined. My canteens were clean, the buttons on my gear were bright and glowing, and my straps were even and clean. By 3:15 in the morning, I was done with my rifle and equipment with 45 minutes left to sleep before a trash can was thrown across the room signaling it was time to wake up.

The last thing I remember before I fell asleep was thinking that Wild Bill's equipment was not as clean as mine. I spent hours cleaning every part of my weapon and every piece of my gear. I knew I would be exhausted the next day, but I could sleep later after I passed my inspection and received my weekend pass.

It was 7:00 AM on Friday morning and it had to be the hottest day in July. There we stood at attention as the Platoon Commander (who was 2 hours late…this is within the military version of fashionably late) came to inspect us. It would be difficult to explain how it feels to stand for 2 hours in the morning sun without any sleep. You are hot, your hands are slipping off your rifle, and your legs are very weak. I was standing behind Wild Bill and in the best place to see the Platoon Commander inspect him. It was going to be great to be this close to watch the Platoon Commander rip into him. Doing everything I could to stay awake and not fall on my face, I began to move my eyes back and forth looking at my fellow candidates. We all looked miserable. The way that the platoon wobbled back and forth, I thought we were standing on a boat in high seas. As I continued to tell myself not to be the first one to fall, I noticed Wild Bill. He was not wobbling back and forth like the rest of us. He actually looked sharp, confident, and had a great command presence. As sharp as he looked, I knew his rifle and equipment were going to get him in trouble. The commander walked up to Wild Bill, asked him a few questions, grabbed his weapon from him, looked at it, tossed it back to him, and went to the next candidate.

I couldn't believe it. He only looked at Wild Bill's rifle for 10 seconds. He didn't look at his pack, his canteens, or the buttons on his gear. He just looked at his rifle. I didn't have time to question what had happen and as I began trying to remember my 4th general order, the platoon commander was in front of me. By this time, I was barely able to stand up. My pack was beginning to slip off and my rifle was so slippery, it felt as though it was covered in butter. The platoon commander saw I was in pretty bad shape. He spent more time with me than Wild Bill, asking me more questions and looking longer at my rifle. He wanted to look at my belt buckle and noticed my boots needed more polish. He gave me a nod and moved to the next candidate. I didn't understand why he spent more time with me than Wild Bill. My equipment and rifle had to be as clean if not cleaner than Wild Bill's equipment and rifle. I just didn't understand, but Wild Bill did.

Wild Bill knew two things: (1) His outward and confident appearance was the most important thing in demonstrating his readiness for the inspection (2) He knew the platoon commander had 39 other candidates to inspect and would only have 30 to 45 seconds with each of us. If he looked sharp, the commander would take that first impression as a sign he was prepared.

You can stay up all night trying to learn everything about your product, but you will never learn it all in one night, a week or even a month. In most cases, your first meeting with the customer will not require you to describe every feature of your product. The most important thing about your first presentation is that your delivery must be direct and with a command presence. Think of what you should know in order to start the sales cycle with a good general overview of your product. Understand the key benefits and features and be able to at a moments notice, stand in front of the president of the company or anyone and recite them. Recognize, just like Wild Bill, that you will not have all day with your customer to go over all your product's features and benefits. Prepare for your "inspection" by making sure that you spend time thinking of the questions that the customer could ask and the amount of time your customer has given you for your meeting. All the remaining inspections I had after the first one were the same and that is probably true for most customer presentations.

Wild Bill reflected a presence that showed a sense of confidence that the platoon commander saw and appreciated. You are a reflection of the company you work for and when you are in front of a customer, you need to convey a "command" presence at all time. Your command presence includes everything from appropriate attire to being on time for all meetings. Have the information that you want to review in an orderly manner and make sure you talk to the customer in a positive and assuring manner. The image you portray to the customer will be the image that the customer has of both you and your company.

Be like Wild Bill and take the right time to prepare for the inspection. If you do this, you will be guaranteed a weekend pass.

POLITICAL SCIENCE TEACHER

Picking electives in college is one of the most dangerous decisions you have to make. My objective was to find one that was easy but one that would provide me enough course credits to maintain or raise my grade point average (G.P.A.). I wanted to find one that fit my schedule, but one that had the right teacher. If I made a mistake and picked the wrong one, I would have to work hard to get a good grade. I decided to take PS 301: a political science class.

At the first class, I sat in the back and observed the other students. My objective was not to determine who was smarter but who choose the class for the same reason I did. I noticed several "electiveteers" in the class and this made me feel my selection was good. But leaving nothing to chance, I had the course catalogue with two alternative classes circled. The instructor arrived and mentioned he would only keep us a few minutes to review the syllabus. This was great. I would have enough time to get back to the fraternity house and play some afternoon poker.

The syllabus was not what I expected. The class would require the reading of 8 books with a paper due for each book, a mid term and final exam. There were even pop quizzes! A college course with pop quizzes? Some of my fellow "electiveteers", wasting no more time listening to the madness, ignored any class room etiquette and left the class to race down to the registration department to get out of the class. I heard them racing down the hall, the echo pitch of their running feet getting farther and farther down the hall until I heard the unmistakable sound of the hall door slam. I wanted to get up and join them but waited until the class was dismissed to begin my journey to the registration line. Though a noble gesture, it served to be my downfall.

As I stood in line behind several familiar faces, I watched the opportunities of an easier class become darker and darker. With the line moving slower and the available seats of my classes getting smaller, I saved myself the agony and torment of waiting to hear that all the other classes were "sold out" and walked back to my room. I could drop it completely, but I would be under the full time student credit limit and would lose part of my tuition. I was stuck with nowhere to go but to PS 301.

As I expected, the class was smaller in numbers. A few of the "electiveteers" recognized each other from being in line trying to get out of the class. We embraced our destiny with a "band of brothers" mentality, sitting together in the back of the class waiting for our fate. The professor walked in. He looked at the size of the class and began handing out the new syllabus. The new syllabus consisted of 3 books to read, 3 papers to write, and a take home final. The best news was there were no pop quizzes! I enjoyed the class, learned something, and got a B. This was one of the best classes I ever took that taught me a great deal about the professor as well as my future customers.

The professor took his job and this class seriously. The other students who left didn't see the value in the class or the professor. There was no reason for the professor to waste his time teaching them about a subject that they had no interest in except to get a good grade with little or no effort. Why waste his time on people who didn't respect both his profession and what he was presenting. He wanted to share his ideas as well as understand the thoughts and opinions presented by his students.

Salespeople make their livelihood on determining what is a good opportunity and one not worth pursuing. We have the responsibility for making our choices and are accountable for the decisions we make. No salesperson should make a choice based on a single piece of information presented by a customer. In some cases, this information could have come from a competitor and may not be true. Just as the professor, customers want to be respected for both their position within their company and their role in making the right decision. This choice includes working with the right people who care. They make the wrong choice, they could be stuck with a sales person who is only looking for the quick and easy sale with little regards for the customer's future needs or concerns after the contract is signed.

Respecting the customer's decision making process and his role will allow you to handle the ups and downs within the sales cycle. Be tenacious and give the customer a chance to test your conviction and loyalty to your product and his business' needs. Remember there are no course catalogues in sales and you can't afford to "drop" too many classes before you boss puts you on double secret probation.

GO FISH

I have never won a deal during a presentation, but I have lost a few when I focused more on what I wanted to tell the audience than on presenting to them what they wanted to hear.

In most cases, your group presentation is probably the only time that everyone will be together in one room. You need to make a great first impression on this group because they are the ones that will make the decision on your product. Your presentation has to be perfect and I have been doing this for such a long time, that I could do my presentation in my sleep. I always find the best place to get lunch and always tip the delivery person a few extra bucks to ensure they stay to help set it up and to bring extra ice. I have the extra pens, the good ones that the nurses like and even some extra mini flash lights so they can bring them home for their kids. I have been doing this for so long; I am even ready for the one guest that is at 99% of all my presentations…. "The guy".

We all know "the guy". The one in the corner who has nothing to do all day and his biggest highlight is getting a free lunch and disrupting your presentation. The guy who you never met before and who gets invited because they want to fill the room with more of them than you. The guy who is first in line to eat, but the last one to thank you for the meal. The first one to complain that it is pizza, but the one that takes the leftovers with him.

You know what I am thinking as he asks the first question. Why is today the day that he has to try to justify why he was invited by asking this stupid question? Couldn't he just eat his pizza and be quiet? What kind of question is that anyway? This guy is slowing me down and embarrassing me in front of the audience. I am going to put him in his place right in front of all his peers. I know everything and I can't afford this guy with the fat tie that now has pizza stains on it to embarrass me or stop me from saying and doing what I want to do.

Everyone in the audience knows it's a stupid question and everyone knows that you know more about your product than he does no matter how many old brochures of your product he has read. How you use and handle this guy in this setting will dictate your success. You are there to help them all learn about the product, even if it means having to answer a stupid question and changing your presentation.

I have a 14 year old daughter. I have played Go Fish (the card game) with her for almost 10 years. I have played about a 1,000 games of Go Fish and I have never won. I have come close to winning, but never won a single game. Why would I enjoy losing all the time?

I lost for several reason. The first was that I wanted to keep her interested in playing. If I kept on beating her over and over again, she would get frustrated and may even want to start playing with someone else. The second reason is by losing, it would give her a chance to understand the game and since she always wins, she will enjoy the feeling of winning and also learn about how to play the game with me. The final reason is that she had to learn how to win. I am playing with her not only to teach the rules of the game, but how to play to win. I think we spend more time teaching our kids how to be good losers than to be great winners. Learning to win is a proactive way of thinking while you are playing the game. Losing is reactive.

"The guy" is the best thing you have going for you! Instead of beating him or showing him up, I welcome the question answering it in a clear and concise manner. If I don't know the answer, I actually use it as a transition to what I want to say. This allows me to keep the flow of my presentation without that "pin drop" silence when a question is answered and you don't know where to resume in your presentation.

This stupid question can also put the audience in a supportive role. There is always one person just waiting to get you on the ropes with a question or issue they have got from your competitor. This may stop him right in his tracks by providing you a golden opportunity to get the audience to see you as a nice guy, committed to working with the audience, and including them in the conversation. You set the tone by being seen as supportive and making "the guy" feel like a winner. You let him know that you appreciate his interest and you are there not as someone who wants to just throw up a PowerPoint presentation and tells everyone to hold all questions to the end, but to make them all "winners" by getting them engaged with their product selection. "That's a great question "guy"; let me try to answer it for the group".

This guy could also be the CEO's best friend. One day he's the guy with the stupid question and the next day he is the guy that is making the decision. In long sales cycle, the players can change often and frequent. Just like with my daughter…one day she is living in my home, the next day she is sending me to the retirement home. The point is that if you treat them with respect and teach them how to and why to win, the new guy in charge of making the decision to buy your product and your kids will look out for you.

I want to leave you with one quick reminder about "the guy" and the stupid question. When I played Go Fish with my daughter, I knew when it was time to quit and play another game. She would do something silly or lose focus. "The guy" can sometimes become more distracting than supportive. Try to limit the number of questions to around three. After the third one, you need to politely tell him that you would be more than happy to stay after the presentation to answer his additional questions. You need to consider the other group and the time that you have to present the information to the rest of the audience. Never lose control and know when it is time to move on.

Take the time in these presentations to help them learn about your product and how to use it. This is not about telling them how much you know about the product as much as it is teaching them how the product will work for them to be successful. If you play your cards right and follow this advice, you will always know when to "go fish".

DIRECTIONS

It is been a long day and you are exhausted from a business meeting that went way too long. You want to get to your room, take off your shoes, go to the bathroom, and have a drink. You have been driving around for 15 minutes and everything looks the same. You finally give in and pull to the side of the road where there is a nice old lady who you hope can give you directions.

She knows exactly where you need to go but unfortunately begins by telling you the first time she went to the hotel and how the lobby was so lovely during that Christmas season. She continues by telling you to go one way and stops herself because maybe it's better, due to the time and traffic, to go another way. She pauses again and then starts reciting street names and counting out loud the number of streetlights you will pass before your next turn. Now you are more confused than you were before you asked her, the cars behind you are blowing their horns and you tell her thank you knowing you have to find someone else to help you. In this situation, the old lady was telling you how to get to the hotel and not giving you directions.

"Telling" and "giving" directions are two different things. Telling directions demonstrates your knowledge of how to get there. There maybe a 100 ways to get to the hotel and some are not as easy as others. Giving directions is the art of explaining how to get there to someone lost and ensuring it is easy and can be remembered. Do you tell advice or give advice? As a salesperson, does your customer expect you to tell them or give them information about your product?

In giving directions, I will always use big landmarks like towers, buildings, or big signs because these are things I notice everyday and are simple to recognize. I always get nervous when someone says to me "a few miles down the road" or "after the third stoplight". I don't do well in figuring mileage as I am driving and always forget when to start counting the stoplights. I also have a hard time reading street signs while I am driving 40 miles an hour with cars behind me.

Your customer needs directions on why your product is better in a clear and concise manner that is easy to remember. It's not how much you tell him, it's how much he understands and retains. Your customer is also getting directions from your competition. This means that he is getting directions from a lot of different people. You have to believe that it is hard to keep up with them all in proper order and sequence.

I have always used a "3 reason" approach. Think of three reasons why your product is the best and consistently remind the customer of these every chance you have in your sales discussion. Make them simple and easy to remember. Think about radio commercials. Did you memorize the words to those silly jingles you hear on the radio? You never wrote them down to study, but I bet if I named one of them, you would know every word. The reason is that they were simple and you heard them often. You will always have a better chance of the customer remembering the "concepts" of what you are saying about your product than every "word" on your brochure or presentation.

Finally, the reason why I hate to ask for directions is because I am admitting to a total stranger I have no control of where I am going. I am lost. Your customer feels the same way when he is "asking" for directions. He is lost and certainly a little defensive having to come to you for help. He wants information he can use and apply in his decision. Just like giving directions, he wants to get there as easy as he can without 10 different street names. Someone usually has to ask for advice before it is given (unless it is my mom) and providing it with the understanding that it took some effort on the customer's part to contact you should be considered a compliment.

Make it a point to make it simple and easy, comprehensive and concise, and with the knowledge that you have been there before and know for certain where he needs to go.

ELECTRIC FOOTBALL

When playing electric football in the Emerson house, there are many rules that you will not find in the rule book that comes with the game. These include the number of players on the field, what determines a complete pass, and how many times you can move your players during the play. Our rules clearly state that the offense could make three moves while the defense was limited to only one. This meant that the defense had to be absolutely sure when to move but the offense had more flexibly. If played correctly, the offense could force the defense to move early in the play. I loved to play electric football, but my brothers only wanted to play if they would win. Any sign that they were going to lose, even if it was the first play, either one would quit. Their "cry baby" excuses sound similar to the ones we hear from our customers. When my brothers would say "You are cheating", it sounded the same as a customer saying "Your product is not as good as the competition". "I am bored and want to do something else" sounds the same as "Your product isn't what I need and I am going with your competition". Finally, "I think Mom is calling me" sounds like "My boss is telling me I need to reevaluate our position and finances before we can commit". Whether it was electric football or checkers (sometimes you let the opponent take/jump one of your pieces to put you in a position to take/jump two pieces from him), the only way to still play or win the deal is to allow your opponent to win at certain times. By controlling when they should win allowed me to play longer with both my brothers and my future customers. The key is to let him win when you want him to win.

Customers are looking to beat you and to get the very best deal. When the customer is ready to start the game, you can usually count on three moves. The customer's first move is the request for the "spreadsheet". The "spreadsheet" has your entire product's information on it so the customer can compare your product with the competition. Later within the sales cycle, you will get the "final pricing" move that is never really the final price, but no one has come up with the name for the price in between budgetary and price on the contract. Finally, if you get to play long enough, you will get the famous "your competitor is a lot cheaper than you" move. This move is usually on a Friday afternoon as you are driving to your in-laws with the kids in the car. Friday is a very tough time to get your boss on the phone to talk pricing and is exactly planned that way by the customer. Let's review each move and how being prepared will allow you to handle these without using a single move.

The first move is the spreadsheet and after sending it to him to review, the customer comes back and tells you that your competition is better. Of course there will be something the competition does better than you. If your product was perfect, they would not need you to sell it. You expected this comment before you even sent him the spreadsheet because you know more about your competition than your customer knows about your product. Just like when playing electric football with my brothers, number 22 is the fastest plastic player on their team. Anyone who played electric football knows that the "hunchback" figure that looks like his hands can't reach his pant pockets is the fastest. You know he will be involved in every play, so focus on him and forget about the quarterback figure (number 12 in our household) that just "spins" in circles when you turn the field on.

Having in place a clear understanding of your competition (or where number 22 was) and your product should help you handle the customer's first move. You discuss the competitor's claims in a clear and concise manner focusing on your positives versus their negatives. If you are not prepared or haven't taken the time to understand the competition and your product, you will lose credibility. If they have to wait too long for your answer, they will get bored with you and want to work with someone else. Having your defense lined up for this one will make the rest of the play easier and not give the customer a sense that you are playing catch up with your competition or acting like the "spinning quarterback".

The next move is usually the "final price" request. Price is one of those things that customers feel they are in absolute control of and gives them a great reason or excuse not to buy your product. Demonstrating the value and security that your product provides before the "move" even starts is essential. Don't lose site that when they ask for final price, you have the control of getting back with an answer. You should be prepared for this by having limits already set. Make a point to review pricing with your team and management as soon as you feel the customer will be selecting a vendor. You don't want to be scrambling around on Friday afternoon, trying to call everyone in headquarters to approve a price that will probably not be the "final" price. You make too many calls to upper management and they begin to wonder if you ever had control of this deal

The final move is the "you are more expensive than the competition" and should be a good sign that they are still interested in playing. Once again, if you are prepared and have lined up your team correctly, you can save your one move. Make it a point to provide assurance that pricing, though important to the customer, is a function of the customer's commitment to you. If you have established a credible and professional relationship, asking for a commitment as vendor of choice before the final pricing is presented is appropriate.

Pricing is objective. A $200,000 difference in price is $200,000 dollars the customer needs to consider when going to the purchasing department or board to ask for the money. If you have been prepared and coached him on the value of your product beyond the price tag, the customer can make the argument that your product is worth the additional dollar amount.

The final move is the close. The customer is getting close to making the decision and has usually narrowed it down to two vendors. The customer needs to know, as he is giving up control in making a selection, that he is getting the most out of the vendor. Head to head comparisons are always subjective with customers. In most cases, there are more similarities than differences between the final two vendor's products and usually at this time, the customer is trying to talk himself out of selecting one vendor rather than convincing himself to select another. The customer wants to win and your final move should let him.

When I played with my brother, I would actually move one of my players away from number 22 (the best player he had). He would spot good old number 22 and throw it to him. With my customer, my one move was a software concession, more discount, or extra training if we can close the deal today. As I mentioned earlier in the "Viva Las Vegas" analogy, I know exactly what I have in place to "give up" before I get too far down in the sales cycle. Just like my defense, I was prepared to give up control when I was ready. I also made sure that I planned it to be the time the customer was ready too!

The customer now has the offer I have presented to him, recognizes this is his time to strike and makes the final move by either giving me the deal or saying I lost it. Either I won the deal or I walk out with nothing left to offer him.

Everyone will tell you a good defense wins championships. Being prepared for the customer's moves is essential. It saves you time, limits confusion, and builds credibility with your customer. If you can control the moves, you let everyone win.

ORANGE

Never under estimate your value to your company and the unique skills and talents you have to be successful as a salesperson. Do you ever wonder why you became a salesperson? I bet if we all got together we would come up with several reasons. There are some who are in sales for the money, the recognition, the trips, or maybe to see how many paper certificates suitable for framing they can get to fill their office wall. There's probably a hundred more that I don't even know, but whatever they are, they all have one thing in common; it's your need to be successful. Success can look different for each of us, but it's all the same. It provides the same feeling of pride and self-esteem whether it is an award you receive in front of your peers or your own individual accomplishments. You know how you feel when you succeed and that sense of accomplishment, but what about your customers and the other people on your team. It would be difficult to try to pick everything that makes your customers feel successful, but that is your job. When you think of your customer's success, think of an orange.

It is a scientific fact that if a 100 people looked at an orange, it would be impossible for any two people to see the same color! The size of their eyes, their height, where they were standing and the light reflecting from their eyes would all create a different color orange to each viewer. However, as long as they kept their eye on the orange, regardless of where they were, they would all be convinced that they see orange.

There are some people who view success by having a large boat or a big house. Some consider success as being the number one sales rep in the company and others just consider success as having a job that pays the bills and allows them to spend more time with their family. Each sales person is keeping his eye on success, but viewing it from a different place.

Your customer is making a very big decision for their company. Most of our sales cycles take a long time. Throughout the course of a sales cycle, your customer will have several places to view his "orange". The customer has several choices where to sit to see the color orange and his success. Each competitor has a special way for him to see it. Your responsibility is to not only get him to see it from your "angle", but to make sure he stays in your seat. The competitor's responsibility is to get your customer in their seat. The longer he sees it from someone else's angle, the more chances he may like it from that view.

Take time with your customer to learn what makes them successful. Their success should go beyond the actual purchase of your product. Sure that's what you are there for, but just as important is how the product will make his job, the company, and his employers successful. This allows you to gain a better knowledge of the customer's present and future expectations of the product and allows you to "direct" him to your place to see his success.

More times than not, your products have more similarities than differences from your competitor. This allows the customer to feel comfortable moving from seat to seat to find the right place to see his success. After some time, the customer will ultimately convince himself that most products will meet his needs. By focusing on his success, you keep him more engaged and allow him to feel more comfortable with both your product and how it will make him successful. Remember, it is all about him!

The orange will never change. The orange will never move. The reason we lose the deal is that the customer has moved to a different place, a different light or different angle from ours. No customer buys a product that he knows will fail, but rather what product does he trust will not fail. Talk about how your product will make him successful; provide a success story for each feature that your product provides going beyond a generic benefit that your brochure shows. Finally, remember in order to appreciate someone's orange you have to see it from their point of view and in doing so, you may see yours as well.

978-0-595-34942-5
0-595-34942-0